Wise to the West

WISE *to the* WEST

POEMS BY
Wendy Videlock

ABLE MUSE PRESS

Able Muse Press

www.ablemusepress.com

Printed in the United States of America

Library of Congress Cataloging-in-Publication Data

Names: Videlock, Wendy, author.
Title: Wise to the West : Poems / by Wendy Videlock.
Description: San Jose, CA : Able Muse Press, [2022]
Identifiers: LCCN 2021060269 (print) | LCCN 2021060270
    (ebook) | ISBN 9781773491134 (paperback) | ISBN
    9781773491141 (ebook)
Subjects: LCGFT: Poetry.
Classification: LCC PS3622.I365 W57 2022 (print) | LCC
    PS3622.I365 (ebook) | DDC 811/.6--dc23
LC record available at https://lccn.loc.gov/2021060269
LC ebook record available at https://lccn.loc.gov/2021060270

Cover image: *Raven Totem 2* by Nancee Jean Busse

Cover & book design by Alexander Pepple

Able Muse Press is an imprint of *Able Muse: A Review of Poetry, Prose & Art*—at www.ablemuse.com

Able Muse Press
467 Saratoga Avenue #602
San Jose, CA 95129

for Sheikh Ma Shieraki Anni

Acknowledgments

The author wishes to thank Alex Pepple for his generous and patient support, and to acknowledge the following journals where these poems, some in earlier versions, first appeared:

Able Muse: "In the Womb You Will Begin to Learn," "O Timothy Tim," and "These Too"

Alabama Literary Review: "And Still"

Fungi Magazine: "Throwing Shade"

Hopkins Review: "Deconstruction" (subsequent appearance in *The Best American Poetry*), "The Inquiry," "Ode to the Slow," "To the Impassioned Poet," "Were You Young Again," and "The Word I Wish to Understand"

Hudson Review: "The Feather" (formerly "The Wren"), "Figures," "Radial Symmetry," "Sevens in the Spring," and "The Summit"

In the Garden (Torrey House Press Anthology): "On Gardening in the West"

Light: "Thirty days without," "Western Wiccan" (formerly "The Wiccan"), and "Wits' End"

Literary Matters: "This Morning in the Shower"

Rattle: "Here in the West," "I have been counting my regrets," "On the Practice of Opine," "Sticks and Sky," and "Thirteen Ways of Looking at a Yellow-Headed Blackbird"

THINK: "Lost Poet at the Barbershop," "Said the old wrangler," "The stark and the spare," and "Whatever the Weather"

Contents

Wise to the West

Stalk the gaps.

—Annie Dillard

Wise to the West

The stark and the spare

and strands

of windswept hair

are always in

abundance

on the desert air.

Like you,

I've been kissed
by tragedy and illness,
by clarity

and clouds of mist, by tiny gifts
and little trees
of amethyst, by bursts

of amaryllis, by anger's fist,
by glimmers
    of forgiveness.

Subject to Erasure

Captains, drop your weapons.
Fathers, show your faces.
Makers, know your pencils

are softened by your natures,
are sharpened by your visions,
are subject to erasures,

are snapped by undue pressure.
Physicians, know your forests.
Sisters, know your natures.

Brothers, mend your pencils.
Mothers, know the sutures
you've tended through the ages.

Teachers, send the mentors
with rivers full of water
and spirits filled with saplings

to fill the books with pages
of mothers with their faces,
of fathers with their sutures,

of nature with its mirrors
of its monsters and its sages.

An Act of Possibility

To open up the heart
may be difficult as a cliché
and might well be an act

of possibility,
the hand of generosity,
a sacred new geometry—
a brave new world

of pitch and luminosity.

Landmarks

Dancers and Dabblers, Makers and Gardeners,
Sisters and Brothers, Under-the-Influence-
of-the-Moon Children of Gratitude,

I write to you from the foot, from the base,
from the sands of a tabletop mountain known to some
as *Mesa Grande*, known to others as *The Grand Mesa*,

to others as the gate to the Rockies,
known to the ancient ones as *Thunder Mountain,
Thiguanawat*, or *Land of the Spirits Long Departed*.

It's said that *wisdom lies in places*.
This red-rock land, once an ancient seaway, has been known
by Allosaurus, Inoceramus, Ute, Hopi, bighorn, lion,

hummingbird, hawk—is shaped by column, terrace, butte,
  bluff,
and blaze, is formed by the roan plateau,
basalt lava flow, slick-rock, globe mallow, Mancos Shale,
  juniper,

and sandstone. This place on earth is also marked by human
  greed
and cruelty, by broken creed and tragedy, by western wind
and sprinklings of recovery. Today this great valley is known

as the place where the peach and grape will grow, is known
for its million-dollar breeze, is known as the confluence
where the Gunny and Colorado Rivers join

and have fallen low. We gather here together in this place,
in this life, in this world to *endure* as William Blake would say,
the beams of love, to deepen our understandings

of currency and cultivation, of language and of cessation,
of story and of invocation, and of time—with its traces
and its wisdom which, it is said, lies in places.

The Horse Next Door

When the horse next door finally died
    I was sure
      I couldn't bear it

for the one left behind.

Learning to Breathe

Suddenly between my ears
a slew of fears
a score of closed
windows and doors
a corridor fraught
with toxic talk
where words produce
within the chest
a panic fest,
a crisis crest—

and

then

the deep breath . . .
an aperture,
the signature

reminder that
the body is home
and a beginning is
the same as
a nonce
form

or a summer
storm—

not an erasure but
a departure

from the norm.

Deconstruction

The chickadee is all about truth.
The finch is a token. The albatross
is always an omen. The kestrel is mental,
the lark is luck, the grouse is dance,
the goose is quest. The need for speed
is given the peregrine, and the dove's
been blessed with the feminine.

The quail is word and culpability.
The crane is the dean of poetry.
The swift is the means to agility,
the waxwing mere civility,
the sparrow a nod to workin'-class

nobility. The puffin's the brother
of laughter and prayer, the starling the student
of Baudelaire. The mockingbird
is the sound of redress, the grackle the uncle
of excess. The flicker is rhythm,

the ostrich is earth, the bluebird a simple
symbol of mirth. The oriole
is the fresh start, the magpie prince
of the dark arts. The swallow is home
and protection, the vulture the priest

of purification, the heron a font
of self-reflection. The swisher belongs
to the faery realm. Resourcefulness
is the cactus wren. The pheasant is sex,
the chicken is egg, the eagle is free,

the canary the bringer of ecstasy.
The martin is peace. The stork is release.
The swan is the mother of cool discretion.
The loon is the watery voice of the moon.
The owl's the keeper of secrets, grief,
and fresh-fallen snow, and the crow
has the bones of the ancestral soul.

And we tell ourselves

the glass
is where we find ourselves.

The Badger

Under the ficus there's a badger
watching me practice yoga.
What have you done
with your wild mind
she asks

and I unbutton
my third eye,
my wild mind,
and my unslaughtered lamb.

Here in the West

Here in the west, whatever
one's pain,
one never complains
about the rain.
What's good for the plains
is bad for harvest.
What freezes in spring
is sugar-beet borrowed.
The river depletes.
The groves expire.
What blooms
in summer is wildfire.

The Summit

Said the lion lying with the lamb,
a life is lived by scent and stem;
the world is full of manic verbs,
ranchers, raptors, dancing birds.

Replies the center of all sound,
I propose the underground.
The stars will open their mouths wide,
suggests the ruler and the slide.

As above so below,
cackles the ordinary crow.
The elk, the shear, and a working wage
are ever in and out of range,

murmurs the little sleeping lamb.
Concurred the wolf, the hawk, and man.
The bowl is destined to provide,
said Doctor Jung and Mister Hyde.

The skin is spent in search of the world,
agreed the mink, the fox, and the girl.
We submit you are not alone,
intoned the moon, and the bird, and the bone.

The sun has only just begun,
the winds will instruct the possessive ones.

Figures

A metaphor is not a wall,
but a turn in the sudden
feel of it all,

the breath that comes
before the fall,
the calm that comes

before the form,
a philosophic
casting call,

a shapely reminder
that language is limber,
thought is a bridge,

the brain is a gate
(which is the break
in its own wall),

and the heart's inclined
to the primal sound
of the undiscovered

waterfall.

The Feminine Principle

The feminine principle,
that underlies the mind,
has no interest in why
a moment becomes magical

and yet it should be said
the feminine principle,
that underlies the mind,
is of the earth, and far more wed

to what within the magical
is tangible, dynamical,
and ultimately whole
                    and enigmatical.

These Too

The fire that burns across the west
and sears into your thumping chest,
the beloved friend to anger wed
who put a gun against his head,
the beautiful one who lost her breast,

the father pretending to remember,
the basil plant that went to seed,
the cat that never shed its fears,
the holiday struck down by disaster,

the invisible internal bleed, the cut,
the clot, the low-lying river,
the annoying eternal dreamer,
the corrupt and smiling preacher,
these too

       are the teacher.

With These Four Words

Fifteen days in hospital
surgeries
and complications
mysteries
and supplications
long and weeping
conversations
various

humiliations
blood-soaked
devastations
pain-filled
bifurcations
wan
and reduced

to providence
and nerve
only to emerge
with these four words

how
can I serve . . .

The unexamined life contains

few birds, no moon,
no slow

-stirred soup.

Lost Poet at the Barbershop

Merrill has owned the barbershop
for twenty-seven years and grew
peaches and apricots before that.

It's what we do in Palisade,
grow some trees, cut some hair,
draw a wage. Then he said

something low and strange about
the kited moon and the blistered page,
the tethered wind, and the river's age.

Feeling a need perhaps to explain
he laughed and said for saying stuff
like that, nobody gets paid—

besides, it's not the kind of thing
people say in Palisade.

In Which the Desert Speaks
on the Subject of Silence

When with an acquaintance or a stranger
or a friend
and words don't arrive or arise or
descend,
one needn't seek filler or
pretend
a little bit of silence is
a horror or
a devastating
end.

This Morning in the Shower

This morning in the shower
the water

was not a means to an end
or a place where
over and over and over again
the mind
worries and plans and frets

but rather the water

was water, and I earth
      and water's
           daughter.

On Gardening in the West

We finally find
we can't divide
the root from fruit
or style, the pit
from heart or guile,
the taste from old
desire.
As we find ourselves
hoping to know
about the way
things will grow,
we discover
the disassembled parts
create a hole—and anyway
it isn't where a row
of beans begins or where
it ends, but whether
midsummer, it
reveals itself
desperate and heat-
strained,
or suddenly
strangely ordained.

Throwing Shade

We think we contain multitudes. . . .
The mushroom contains multitudes
and has something to do
with the influence of the moon.

The mushroom is ever the secret reaper,
the hermit, the healer, the deep wood sage.
It grows in the dark and throws shade.

The mushroom is present as the Buddha,
is of another age, is of another Eden,
is ancient and all the rage.
The mushroom contains multitudes
and multiplies, is wedded to the bride
and the groom, the moment and
the multiverse, the water,
and the garlic and the spoon.

The mushroom is both overlooked
and sought, like a precious jewel.
The mushroom, quiet-like,
defies,
and defines the wise—it contains
multitudes
        and multiplies.

The Inquiry

Who left it there, the child asked, while gazing
at the harvest moon rising over the butte.
What could I say that wouldn't turn her wonder
into something tied up in a knot of words
she'd know at once to be a lie? That rock
which glows contains not a shred of light.
Dear child, illusion is a lovely sight.
Reflection and wonder is the only Christ.
One day you'll swim across the sky and touch

her face, for she is one of many mothers
of you and she watches over the great big world—
she grows large and grows slender over
the earth for you. That which is false also
is true. *All mothers and moons know this to be true.*

A Preference

Though it can be
delicious
to board the ship
of fierce and feverish

it's mostly pretty
lecherous
and certainly
ungenerous

to one's wider frame
of reference
and one's holy
and adventurous

row row rowing of
the humble boat
of temperance.

On the Practice of Opine

So many blessings,
so many complaints—let's
be honest, if
opinion

were a religion
we'd all be saints.

Given a Choice

Today I was given a choice:
consumption or creation.

I chose an old ball of string
and all morning long

I played with the cats.
I did not look at the clock.
I did not answer my phone.

Something was taking form.

I noted it was an awful lot

like writing a poem.

On Becoming a Nowist

So there I was, pushing a wheelbarrow
up a hill, thinking a little about Sisyphus,
a little about the glazed rain

-water, a little of Monty Python
and the not yet dead, and I wondered

what on earth do others think about
when pushing a wheelbarrow
up a hill?

Suddenly ramming into a rock and nearly
spilling into the wheelbarrow,
I've come to believe
most people are likely concentrating

on the fucking wheel.

On Hearing Yet Another Person Say They Haven't Got a Creative Bone in Their Body

And yet you've spent your entire life
creating—you've spent your life
                    making—
making dinner, making drinks,
making fire, making
the cut, making amends,
making fun,
making the team,
making money, making
lemonade

of lemons, yes, we spend
our whole lives making—
making decisions,
making peace,
making war,
making mistakes,
making a call, making some
        kind
            of sense of it all—

we can't help but spend our lives making
        music, making choices,
making strides, making up

for lost time,
making hay and haste,
and promises and progress,
making love, making
history, making
predictions, making
productions, making
light

of the situation,

we make space,
we make friends,
we make magic, we make trouble,
we make mountains

out of molehills,

we make tea,
we make tracks,
we make use, we make do,
we make way, we make curds,
we make words, we make waves
we make meaning—
  we are born

into this world and are made

for making, making, making.

Solstice Child

It's true that you emerged from the root
cellar of the world, strewn
    with straw and wet of womb.
  It's true that you were brought

by the stars and delivered by moon,
surrounded by jazz and wrapped
in the blues, storied
by forests and sanded by dunes,

it's true that you are the sonic boom
and the tablespoon, the certain and
    the never presume, the river's curve
and the river's canoe, the light

of the bride and the dark of the groom,
the still point and the mystery school.

Whatever the Weather

Give me a lever . . . and I shall move the world.
—Archimedes

Neither naked nor clad,
I bring my angel
to the water, float her over

the memory of my old
country father,
a long-estranged

mother
and daughter,
a catatonic brother.

An angel is
nothing like a savior,
is nothing like a lever

but is practiced in the tides,
is familiar with all weather.
Disillusion's favored lover

straddles the divide,
balances another
broken set of saviors and

a legendary lever at
an unexpected curve in the river.

In the womb you will begin to learn

the ways of water, although its warmth

may lead you to its mysteries,

its formlessness and changing forms,
its seeds and beads

and underbellies, its freezes and complexities,
its fogs and rippling memories,

its whisperings and crashings through—

but what is strangely beautiful

    is what the water teaches you

is sordidly or splendidly
                or depressingly up to you.

Touch

When the world and I
appear at odds
and body is

estranged

from mind
and heart
is all asunder

it's good to remember

just how little
(and then

how much)
the horse next door

came to trust
        my touch.

Sevens in the Spring

It's said the more alive you are the more
you stumble. It's also said
what doesn't kill you makes you humble.
The doe-eyed doe and the sparrow have sent
the oriole to remind me
I haven't filled the feeder. Belief
in anything omnipotent beyond the singing bird

is bound to bring a heckle, or
a long-awaited stutter. In the ravine
an evergreen's been planted in your name.
It spreads its limbs, and limber is,
and even seems to catch a joy
as it flies, and still, it's not the same.
Perhaps the rebellious revel in

the deathbed the way one revels in
the news, or the blues, or the warmth
of the ordinary clutter. Perhaps
we're all just orphans, seeking wheat
and butter. In the ravine, my dear old friend,
a trace of snow. An evergreen.
The ghost of a ghost of a doe.

Hey, Dad,

remember the time
you caught me writing

you asked what I was doing

I said I was writing a letter
to Gram and Grandad Joe

I was really writing a poem.

Why

Said the brother with a boulder on his shoulder
when the world is full of wonder
    why should I have to suffer

Said the father of the bride and the tie
of the groom why should I
    say anything to change your loony tune

Said the little elder sister why should I
warn the others
why should I keep an eye

Said the moon to the tide said the brood
    to the broody why should I
become the teacher

why am I my brother's keeper
why should I become occluded
why is consciousness avoided
why is learning not included

said the righteous or disputed,
why should I learn anything

I know
you think I'm stupid.

Land of the Free

for JB

You can change the laws
but you can't change me.
We who believe

in the home of the brave,
we who believe
in the land of the free

are free,
free, free
to poison honeybees.

One needn't be seen

to be heard said the aspen leaf

or was it the bird?

Whatever It Is

*You would think that these rich colors reside
in the thing itself, that the cactus, the crayons,
the lichen* have *their colors. But colors are not
possessions; they are the intimate revelations of
an energy field.*

—Ellen Meloy

One calls it the opening
another says

a softening

another would say
it's a weakening

another yet
a strengthening,
whatever it is
it's a fleeting thing

freeze thaw

freeze thaw

this is the learning
this is the law
of everything,

of paradox,
the mason's fox,
the genius, and
the box of rocks—
that is the law

intoned the butte,
the yucca stalk,
the rough-hewn,
the bright and glowing
outcrop.

Many Camps

From the long sound of winter to the mythologic spring
to the messy sounds of fall to the current sounds of war

the great bonfire of all

is the one which appears in the morning and makes its way
across the sky. I've heard it said poetry is a way

of getting friendly with your own mind,

of waking the first and third eye, of making a way
across a shared sky, a way of rubbing sticks together,

a way of gathering under the weather,

a way of never saying never. A bonfire, they say, is a way
of getting friendly with the shared mind, of waking the first

and third rhyme, of letting go the omnipresent *why,*

why, why, of making our way across the sky, a way
of learning over and over again many rivers, one water,

many robes, one fiber,
many camps, one fire.

Radial Symmetry

for Chrissy

Today I was given a sand dollar,
another soft reminder
of the earth's difficult birth.
This bone-colored circular form is no stranger

to the palm of my hand.
A velvet-petaled, skim-and-burrow
deep-sea creature becomes this:
a sun-drenched
clean design, conjuring thoughts

of transformation
and the sublime. At the heart
of the five-pointed star
five even tinier pores, where
the architecture

of the world appears to surge.
And should you crack
this fragile shell in half, as all
sea-children come
to learn,
five small doves emerge.

Thirty days without

a cigarette.

I haven't
murdered

anybody yet.

Thirteen Ways of Looking at
a Yellow-Headed Blackbird

I

The sky is falling.

II

Across a dozen hungry nations
it was a large part
of the conversation.

III

In the small northern town
of Chihuahua nothing
is falling
except a thousand
yellow-headed
blackbirds.

IV

I was of ten thousand minds
and twenty
thousand wings.

V

The yellow-headed blackbird
and the fall and the melting sun
swept across
the inside of the eye's horizon

VI

I do not know which is more
disturbing, the murmur or
the sudden slaughter, Moses
or the water parting.

VII

Said the falcon in Chihuahua,
there was only one
yellow-headed blackbird.

VIII

Said the sweeper of the street
in Chihuahua,
there were fifty thousand
yellow-headed blackbirds.
Said the merchant, there was no
time to process three

thousand bolts of electricity
or the satellite
with its scraping sound.

IX

Said the yellow-headed blackbird,
there is the question
of the sky,
the answer of the earth,
and the fiery swoop
of following the leader.

Said another, there is also
the unforgiving pavement
and its unquiet people.

X

O peering little
hungry ghosts,
why do you steep
in your gardens filled
with grievances?
Do you not see
you are the yellow-
headed blackbird,
the water

that is parting,
the starving
conversation?

XI

I cannot stop thinking about shadows
as the yellow-headed blackbird
stammers and pitches and wings
out of sight. The falcon
has filled his belly.
      We watch from our gardens,
remaining piqued and hungry.

XII

The winter is dying.
The spring must be dreaming
of yellow-headed blackbirds.

XIII

It was auburn all afternoon
and all the trees were purple.
The words had turned to scarlet
and the story crept under the bed.
The yellow-headed blackbird,
wet-feathered and sky-laden,
lay curled inside her egg.

Code Switch

When my son finally came out,
he did not say, *Mom, I'm gay,*
but rather, *Mom, you know
I'm gay, right?*

And when my mother heard
the news, she said nothing,
except she'd *never, ever use*

that appropriated word.

To the Impassioned Poet

A vivacious and loquacious
linguistic little trickster,
an underrated consonant,
a solar-powered vowel,
an epic, a ballade, a lyric,

a lynx, the seventh sea, and a bird-
like literary fixture in the form
of an extended metaphor
walk into a bar.

On the wall a burnt-out
lightbulb, a sprig of sage,
an old horseshoe.

There is soup and there is stew.

The rest is up to you.

Said the old wrangler,

There's coffee in the lodge,
a snake in the pit,
some dogs on the loose

and a leak in the roof where
something akin
to sympathy seeps in.

The husband under

an August moon,

playing Bejeweled.

The Word I Wish to Understand

The word I wish to understand
is opaque. The buried
or unexamined

is not the same as the clean slate.
An opal is sometimes real,
sometimes fake—

one vaguely knows a thing
has changed its shape.
I suspect

an accumulation
is what makes an ache.
Sometimes all a word

can do is break
and wait for something to illuminate.

The Quiet Wild

Of books and succulents
    and bits of silhouette,
they've built their elder nest
here at the world's edge.
A heron flies over and she swears
there
is everywhere,
  and nowhere
and then there are the sticks
    in the quiet, wild west.

The Feminine Ending

From India
to Africa
to the roads
of old America,

the seeding
of hepatica,
the chantry
of Ganesha,

the dawning of
ahimsa,
the coming
    of Amen-ra.

Arse Poetica II

You should know your fate is one in which
        the road will turn and twist your arm
or break your heart or a word will rise
a dragon's head or the storm will grow
        to hurricane lengths and somewhere down
the line something shockingly *amor*
fati will come of it—

from the ludicrous to the sublime,
the end rhyme is all about time:
        the volta isn't just for sonnets—mine
for gold and come up onyx—shifts
and sudden shafts of light occur
in these deep dark seas
        of naked receptivity.

There are few words

more sublime

than *once upon a time.*

Ritual

With an old brass bowl,
a braid of sage
and millennia

of love
and rage, we smudge
our home, our feet,

our tongues,
our apparitions
and intentions, our poisons

and corrections,
our legacies of mercy
and contention.

I have been counting my regrets:

bacon, Facebook, cigarettes.
Anger. Bluster.
Laziness.
Fearfulness.
Indifference.
Lousy lovers, stupid bets.

Things that should not be confessed.

I'm still not dead.
It should be said
I haven't finished counting yet.

A Thousand Ticking Clocks

The child raised in the house of anger knows
a thousand ticking clocks, knows the heart
as the door that's always locked, knows
that even the walls are secretly taking stock

and keeping track, knows the tiptoe and
the balanced rock, knows the escape route
and the aimless walk—she knows the double knot
that grows inside the throat, the fire that burns

within the gut, the fear residing where
the light gets in—and knows in her bones wherever
she goes, the miracle hoax and catacomb
from the liquid face of the open road

and the unmistakably warm glow
of the miraculously gracious home.

And Still

I can be knee-deep in poor me,
on a whim, sky high
or medium,

frumpy, glumpy, full
of grandeur,
wracked

with candor, showing
all my years,
grinding

all my gears, bumbled
as a bee,
consumed

with some idea,
and still, you give to me
a tender

kind of sigh,
a slant kind of rhyme,
those

I
-love-you eyes.

Quaran Time

All's quiet on the western slope,
and everywhere
the people are learning
to live with less.

Or

more.

Amor fati

for Jack

This morning during a sudden pang
of missing you I went to a place
        of gratitude

for how you served
as trickster, kin, teacher, fuse,
squatter, grifter, drifter,
muse,
cranky wizard, lady luck,
clutter, clatter,

cluster fuck, captain of the way
things are, dreamer of
the north star, showing us all

to fear is not the same
        as to love
your fate,

and steering

is not to sail, or float,
        or navigate.

On Ceremony

Rituals, anthropologists will tell us, are about transformation.
　　—Abraham Verghese

In winter the house
of grief deepens.
Down

in the dark earth,
small mouths sipping.
Someone

reading, someone
seeking some
kind

of feeling. Some kind
of healing.
A child has eyed

a star

-spangled banner,
the gray dove's
feather,

another bleak
scandal. There,

in the window, someone
burns
a solitary candle.

More or Less

for Rosemerry

In a dusty town somewhere out west,
    down the old land's end,
past the quarry's edge,
at dusk, and dawn, more
or less, comes the woman in
the long red dress.

Up the wooden stair, down the snow-
    deep slope, through the orchard floor
of rot and hope, from the mountain air
and the watercress,
comes the woman with the riven voice,
comes the woman in the long red dress.

From the wrecking ball to the cold compress,
from the lullaby to the wedding chest,
from the child's bed to the brambled

and the dispossessed,

comes the woman in the long red dress,
comes the woman broken
open and infinitely blessed.

To the coal-train towns and the moneyed rest,
to the widowed and the childless,
to the earthy firm
    and the raven's nest,

from the squawking place
   to the unexpressed,

at dusk and dawn, from wheat to chaff,
from soul to soul,
      for more, or less,

comes the one who sings for all the rest,
for the stubborn and the acquiesced,
for the dullard and the sorceress,

for the wild aster in the grass,
for the bodied and the bodiless,
comes the woman in the long red dress.

Minor Adjustment

There aren't any
    Freudian slips,
  but moving seas
    and ghost ships,
     perhaps

designed

to nick
   or realign
     the rudders of
       the honest mind.

On Learning to Relax

I'm learning and I'm practicing
but I confess

I've always found
relaxing
somewhat taxing.

Sitting Still

One wonders what to do
with the nagging thought
that I should be doing
anything
other than learning how to sit.

(Says the yogi,
Notice it.)

A Ring of Ocotillo

*The landscape of the American West has to be
seen to be believed and has to be believed to be
seen.*

—N. Scott Momaday

Long ago she came to know
the sand in the sand
-stone formation, the ghost
in Antelope Canyon,
the dust that surrounds
the old Shell station
where rings of ocotillo tell
a difficult and sage
-filled narration
and a paloverde-dry
river basin on
the Arizona side
of Navajo Nation.

Walking uphill,

taken aback

by the breath I lack.

May all your guardians be with you:

the jester,
the sage, the warrior,
raven and dove
and reaper—
        and remember

every song
has its spring
and each gate
        its gatekeeper.

Western Wiccan

It was hot and late in the morning
when a silent little Kevorkian
arrived in the form of a scorpion.

I couldn't help but think

how like a small accordion,
how like the pale historian—
this dusty desert champion,

this crawling valedictorian,
though startling,
is not so very alien.

And then,

I couldn't help but think
this lost and lonely veteran,
this one who could be anyone,

this delicate Kevorkian
has no business in my room,
and slowly, very carefully

went to fetch my broom.

O Timothy Tim

i.m. Tim Murphy

O Timothy Tim, you dappled thing,
all bard and earth
and vice and hymn, all love

of word and life and limb.

O Timothy Tim.
O Brother Tim,

all unrelenting drive
and whim, all gathering,
and great divides,

all mountain and
all sea and wind,
all staying true

from birth
to death, and back again,
to what's without
and what's within.

About the interwebs,

it could be said
nuance
is dead,

irony's
on oxygen,
satire

is redundant,
but fervor

soldiers on.

The Feather

*Hast thou attuned thyself to the sufferings of
humanity, O candidate for light?*
  —Madame H. P. Blavatsky

The dark guardian of the west
has left a feather in the ash
and given me another test.
The hour gleams and comes to pass.
The winter people send the ghost
of childhood to guard the path.
I'm asked if I am of the coast

or mountain clan. If I should have
an answer, it is in the sand.
My father's hand, my mother's prayers,
my brother's fears, my sister's cage
appear and disappear again.
They light as gull, hook, crow, and wren.

There Are Those

There are those
who find it wrong
to speak of mother trees,
black holes, roan foals,
the dandelion lawn,
or the swallow's song,
and not make stark note
          a war is on.
Alas, again.
Whatever the age a thing
is written, consider this
          a given.

The Cottonwood Plateau

There are things I wish I didn't know.
A moment of syntactic grace
is as the leaves before the snow,
who learn the art, if nothing else,

of turning, and of letting go.
The ancient one who's underneath
the cottonwood is still aglow
with something smacking of belief.

No wind so fierce it blanches crow!
She says this every time we meet
here at the cottonwood plateau.
She looks to me, and doesn't speak

of turning or of letting go.
We leave one another to what we know.

Rhyme, What Good Is It?

for Joshua Mehigan

Well,
I wouldn't wanna kiss it—
it's illicit
it's illegal said the scholar,

said the weasel,
said the anger it inspires,
said the shady and the slanted,

they are sick, they are twisted
(those who bow down
and kiss it)—

quoth the fable with
  a flourish,
    it's okay if it's implicit,

it's the garlic in the biscuit—
they are fascists, they are wicked
(those who stoop
to revere it),
goddess bless
the rhyme-driven, said

the vowel, said the riven,

said the salt in the season
and the bolt in the lightning,
said the shift

in rhythm—it's all good it's all play

said the butter, said the bread,
said the bawdy, said
the dead, said the pollen

of the hour, said the grain
in the word and its weird
little power,

juxtaposed and engendered,
paired up

or neatly slaughtered,
slammed shut, or long remembered,
knotted up or grand

-daughtered, from candlestick

to stream,

how life is but a dream.

Under the Rocks

The gifts we find under the rocks
of the conscious mind
are gifts that bind

the tender ties
and loose the noose
from round the neck:

a stillness,
an unexpected swiftness,
a bout of sudden

genius—or witlessness—
a necessary
restlessness,

the dawning of forgiveness.

A Few Things We Learned from
Our Friend Dale

To live in grace is to die in grace.
A song is better than a thousand books.
Humility is the bottomless bowl.
Where rivers meet, renew your vows.

Meet everybody where they are.
Generosity is the guiding star.
To listen is a skill that has
an eager heart and warm hands.
A belly laugh is a beautiful thing.
To swing on a swing is a dying man's dream.

The weight that you were born to bear
will glean from the soul and take to the air.
There's a hidden path in the wild rye.
It's not so bad having to die.
The hardest part is saying goodbye.

Sticks and Sky

I am steeped in the sticks and stuck on the sky.
The sky is wider than a Twitter feed.
Unplugged for a spell I'm reminded why

to overfeed is to sleep with a capital lie.
The sparrow prefers a world that is wide and treed.
I am steeped in the sticks and stuck on the sky,

and drawn to the root where the river runs dry.
The sound of the rain is a scattering seed.
Unplug for a spell and you'll understand why

what you feed is the same as what you buy.
We're given the frontal lobe and the slow bleed.
I am steeped in the sticks and stuck on the sky—

a crescent moon and the stars are my Fourth of July.
The sparrow prefers an action to a creed.
Unplug for a spell and you'll understand why

it's good to be found outside the public eye.
To learn the difference between word and deed.
I am steeped in the sticks and stuck on the sky;
unplug for a spell and you'll understand why.

If You Believe a Stranger

If you believe a stranger
is a person who
has nothing at all
to do with you, perhaps
it's true, perhaps

it's true you are no fool,
perhaps the moon and the sea
have nothing whatsoever
to do with you, and the greens

and blues, the seed and womb,
and all the creeds and greed
and weeds and blooms,

and all the grief and songs
that stir and fill the world

have nothing to do with you, too.

Were You Young Again

Child, were you young again,
I would bring you bread and jam,
the broken glove, and the promised land.
A pentacle to scuff the sand.
A year of fire to melt your symbols.
Down by the weighted, murky river
is the way that is known by the wolf,
the crane, and the Yeatsian fiddle.

This is no whim. This is not a riddle.
We are a strange and an old people—
the winds that blow through the seat
of the soul and into the stem
of the old reptilian bone disturb
and console, disturb and console.

Wits' End

I will slam my own
hand in the door

and swear off the world
of women and men

if I hear the word
impactful again.

The Dying of the Mother Tongue

for Sherman

A child is born unto this world.
She brings with her the skin
that has been given her, the grievance
that's bequeathed her,
and a gift that has been offered her.
From these things, the child forms
early on a secret code
that might in fact be better known
as scorpion, or bear, or prayer,

or perhaps a kind of living law.
Heredity claims the shape of the jaw.
Geography shapes the palm of the hand.
The dying of the mother tongue
punctuates the northern star,
while destiny stands in the wings
in awe. It's said all laboring
in service of soul is done in the dark,
that nothing's truer than a field

in a breeze, and the life of the mind
is best described
as a kind of collective dream. The skin
of the child who shifts her destiny

is mottled as the moth, is storied
as the mother tree,
and bears the unmistakable mark
of violence and legacy,
of tenderness and melody,
where gift and grief and forgiveness form
a kind of solidarity,
and the closest the gifted child comes
to medicine or remedy.

The Jack of Spades

The old poet, with a flourish, tossed
his book into the flames.
After the shock
had waned, he stood
and said, Yes,

friends,

context
        is everything.

It being winter,

I have been thinking

of Himalayan poppies

and intellectual honesty,

while pondering, as a matter
of course, rights

and responsibilities.
At the crazy prow of my own ship,

I have glimpsed
the dance of the rain in a grain of sand,

a grape of bronze and aquamarine,

a murder of thieves,
a band of angels, and
a pattern upon which it seems

everything is hinged.
And still, I do not understand

if I've discerned the pattern

or the fringe, the organ or

some invisible plan, the fingertip

or the span of my own hand.

Ode to the Slow

I have an affinity for ghosts, and so,
dwelling as we ghostly do, with the caw
and the screech and the pinyon moon, where the freeze
and the thaw and the witness are
together alive and together entombed,
here on the edge of a high desert world
where all is stone, and all is sky,

here where an ancient sea surged forth
and slowly died, here where the ruins and the peaks
have changed their names to butte and bluff,
here where the Ute slowed their feet
and harvested the sister seeds,
here where the reach of the canyon ends
or begins, or infers—like knowledge, it's always

a rapture or a bit of a blur—one could soar on the wing
or fall in—here where the rolling stone knows
the world is only made of sand and the arc
is the mark of the fallen star,
here where the ghosts and the slopes are wan
and empty of virtue and of sin, I lower a bridge
and watch the morning fog roll in.

WENDY VIDELOCK lives on the western slope of the Colorado Rockies with her husband and their assorted critters. Her work appears in *Hudson Review, Oprah Magazine, Poetry, Dark Horse*, the *New York Times, Best American Poetry*, and other venues. Her books are available from Able Muse Press, and her upcoming collection of essays and haibun, *The Poetic Imaginarium: A Worthy Difficulty* (Lithic Press), will appear in mid-2022.

ALSO FROM ABLE MUSE PRESS

Jacob M. Appel, *The Cynic in Extremis: Poems*

William Baer, *Times Square and Other Stories; New Jersey Noir: A Novel; New Jersey Noir (Cape May): A Novel; New Jersey Noir (Barnegat Light): A Novel*

Lee Harlin Bahan, *A Year of Mourning (Petrarch): Translation*

Melissa Balmain, *Walking in on People (Able Muse Book Award for Poetry)*

Ben Berman, *Strange Borderlands: Poems; Figuring in the Figure: Poems*

David Berman, *Progressions of the Mind: Poems*

Lorna Knowles Blake, *Green Hill (Able Muse Book Award for Poetry)*

Michael Cantor, *Life in the Second Circle: Poems*

Catherine Chandler, *Lines of Flight: Poems*

William Conelly, *Uncontested Grounds: Poems*

Maryann Corbett, *Credo for the Checkout Line in Winter: Poems; Street View: Poems; In Code: Poems*

Will Cordeiro, *Trap Street (Able Muse Book Award for Poetry)*

Brian Culhane, *Remembering Lethe: Poems*

John Philip Drury, *Sea Level Rising: Poems*

Rhina P. Espaillat, *And After All: Poems*

Anna M. Evans, *Under Dark Waters: Surviving the* Titanic: *Poems*

Stephen Gibson, *Frida Kahlo in Fort Lauderdale: Poems*

D. R. Goodman, *Greed: A Confession: Poems*

Carrie Green, *Studies of Familiar Birds: Poems*

Margaret Ann Griffiths, *Grasshopper: The Poetry of M A Griffiths*

Janis Harrington, *How to Cut a Woman in Half: Poems*

Katie Hartsock, *Bed of Impatiens: Poems*

Elise Hempel, *Second Rain: Poems*

Jan D. Hodge, *Taking Shape: Carmina figurata; The Bard & Scheherazade Keep Company: Poems*

Ellen Kaufman, *House Music: Poems; Double-Parked, with Tosca: Poems*

Len Krisak, *Say What You Will (Able Muse Book Award for Poetry)*

Emily Leithauser, *The Borrowed World (Able Muse Book Award for Poetry)*

Hailey Leithauser, *Saint Worm: Poems*

Carol Light, *Heaven from Steam: Poems*

Kate Light, *Character Shoes: Poems*

April Lindner, *This Bed Our Bodies Shaped: Poems*

Martin McGovern, *Bad Fame: Poems*

Jeredith Merrin, *Cup: Poems*

Richard Moore, *Selected Poems;*
The Rule That Liberates: An Expanded Edition: Selected Essays

Richard Newman, *All the Wasted Beauty of the World: Poems*

Alfred Nicol, *Animal Psalms: Poems*

Deirdre O'Connor, *The Cupped Field (Able Muse Book Award for Poetry)*

Frank Osen, *Virtue, Big as Sin (Able Muse Book Award for Poetry)*

Alexander Pepple (Editor), *Able Muse Anthology;*
Able Muse: A Review of Poetry, Prose & Art (semiannual, winter 2010 on)

James Pollock, *Sailing to Babylon: Poems*

Aaron Poochigian, *The Cosmic Purr: Poems; Manhattanite*
(Able Muse Book Award for Poetry)

Tatiana Forero Puerta, *Cleaning the Ghost Room: Poems*

Jennifer Reeser, *Indigenous: Poems; Strong Feather: Poems*

John Ridland, *Sir Gawain and the Green Knight (Anonymous): Translation;*
Pearl (Anonymous): Translation

Stephen Scaer, *Pumpkin Chucking: Poems*

Hollis Seamon, *Corporeality: Stories*

Ed Shacklee, *The Blind Loon: A Bestiary*

Carrie Shipers, *Cause for Concern (Able Muse Book Award for Poetry)*

Matthew Buckley Smith, *Dirge for an Imaginary World*
(Able Muse Book Award for Poetry)

Susan de Sola, *Frozen Charlotte: Poems*

Barbara Ellen Sorensen, *Compositions of the Dead Playing Flutes: Poems*

Rebecca Starks, *Time Is Always Now: Poems; Fetch, Muse: Poems*

Sally Thomas, *Motherland: Poems*

Paulette Demers Turco (Editor), *The Powow River Poets Anthology II*

Rosemerry Wahtola Trommer, *Naked for Tea: Poems*

Wendy Videlock, *Wise to the West: Poems; Slingshots and Love Plums: Poems;*
The Dark Gnu and Other Poems; Nevertheless: Poems

Richard Wakefield, *A Vertical Mile: Poems; Terminal Park: Poems*

Gail White, *Asperity Street: Poems*

Chelsea Woodard, *Vellum: Poems*

Rob Wright, *Last Wishes: Poems*

www.ablemusepress.com